Hues Of Black And White

White

A Collection of Poetry

Jenna Cervantes

Made with ❤ on the BookLeaf Publishing Platform

www.bookleafpub.in

www.bookleafpub.com

Dedication

My Dearest Aunt Donna, Thank you for believing in me and encouraging me to create this book, I love you!

To my beautiful children, Hannah, Janelle, and Christian — every word I write is for you. You are the light in my life, the reason I push forward, and I will dedicate all my books to you as a reminder of my endless love and gratitude.

To my mother — you taught me that strength doesn't need to be loud. Through your quiet resilience and grace, I've learned to observe, endure, and grow.

To my brilliant and beautiful sisters, Sara and Kimberly — from the very beginning, you have been my greatest allies and confidants. Your love and support have carried me through every challenge, and I am forever grateful to share this journey with you.

And to my brother Abelito — though you may be far away, your love and support has always been with me. You've been there for me in spirit, and your presence in my life means more to me than I can express in words.

Preface

This collection of poetry, represents an intimate journey into a world of Borderline Personality Disorder (BPD). For many, life is experienced in shades —where emotions and experiences blend, shift, and fade. But for those of us who live with BPD, the world can be more stark, more defined. It is often felt in extremes: in the black of despair and the white of hope, with little room for anything in between.

Through these poems, I seek to bridge the gap between those extremes, to explore the complexities of a mind and heart often at war, and to find the balance, however fleeting, that exists in the middle. These words are mine but speak to anyone who has ever felt trapped by their own emotions, lost in the intensity of their inner world, or disconnected from the understanding of others.

Each poem is a snapshot of a moment in time—some beautiful, some painful, they capture the dualities, contradictions, and nuances that shape life with BPD. My hope is that these poems bring comfort, validation, and perhaps even a deeper understanding of the intricacies of this condition.

Thank you for walking this path with me, for listening to these echoes of my soul. May these words remind us that even in the darkest of times, there is always hope.

—Jenna Cervantes
@mellowdaffodil

Acknowledgements

To all who suffer with BPD, this is for you. I see you, I understand the pain, there is hope in recovery.

1. BlackAndWhite

I go all in for things
If I love you
I love you all the way.
If I hate you,
I hate you the same.
There in no in-between land,
I'll take it as far as I can stand.

2. Splitting

I care
Until I don't
It's called **SPLITTING**
Black or white
No in-between
While I loved you dearly before;
it is a new day
just like that
it is gone.
Like you
like us.
Never-was.

3. My Soul's Dear John

I feel my soul escaping my body;
I find myself gasping in deeply attempting to hold it in.
Trying my best to siphon it back inside to keep it from
drifting into the atmosphere.
One too many times,
like today
I pray and I pray,
That I will not wake up to another goodbye I've gone
away.

4. Vanish

I want to leave
And go far away from here
I will not hear echos from the past
I want a fresh start
No one will recognize my face
I will throw it all away
I will create a new life
I will go by a new name
Nothing will remind me
Because nothing will be the same

5. Much Ado Acerca de Nada

I've been thinking a lot about me-
the things that make up the core of my being.

I have been wondering...
Have I ever been in love?
Sifting through the details of....was it enough?

If I am unsure, does that mean no?
Or am I overthinking each connection as a whole-
a whole, like 100 percent,
or
a hole, like empty space...
Because nothing occupied the place.

6. The Way I Nourish Myself These Days

I sigh and I realign myself,
I am at the center of my universe;
I hold the power of my happiness.
Things come and go.
I remain.
Brilliantly strong and unwavering.
I allow myself to feel everything deeply;
I stand on it until it becomes vapor.
Then I collect the water molecules
Into a tiny flask and drink.
I nourished my body with all the pain and discomfort I
sorted through.

7. Longing for Familiar Virtues

Rigidly exposed on trembling knees
I wonder where have you gone?
Seeking to fill the empty space that lingers where you
were.
Grasping for things that are good chaste and up-
building.
I grope longingly seeking for you, Jah,
and I know you are not near.
Bring me back to where you are.
Bring me back to the safety of your right hand of
righteousness.

8. Rumination

I thought about razor blades
Silver and Crimson
Gliding seamlessly over my skin
I remembered the feeling
of being stretched this thin
It's too late to explain
Turn emotional pain
into a scarlet stain
Let it drip my cares away
Until I let it all go
Until my world turns gray
The shade perfectly centered between black and white
Where I no longer have any strength left to fight.

9. Saguaro

Do not step foot
into the sanctuary I built-
stone by stone,
tear by tear-
after you left.

I remember the table,
salt-streaked and splintered,
"what if"
became my only prayer.

Those days are buried-
the ache of unraveling,
learning to hold myself together
in hands that trembled.

I was a cactus-
thorned and thirsty,
surviving on very little.

But even the desert blooms
when no one is watching.

Even the sharpest things cradle life in their center.

I bloom still-
beautiful, alone-
and without permission.

10. Building Endurance

Existing here proves I can survive anything.
It had slipped my mind for a moment,
the impact of what being here meant.
Then I recall the loneliness....
Then I recall the moments of desperation....
Then I remember all the tears,
all the hard work and dedication;
the simple moments of pride and of shame
of struggle and of fear.
Then.....
I remembered exactly why I am here.

11. Depreciated

My emotions were burdens
I locked them inside
I took the pain out on myself
with razor blades and knives.
I had to be smart I had to be strong
I had to agree
or I was in the wrong.
I must be good
is what I was taught
love is not free
love is bought.
I didn't have anything
you valued very much
for your attention
I was out of luck.
Be seen and not heard is what you said
I kept myself busy wishing I was dead.
I found you in the men I have loved
who belittle and neglect me
who abuse and judge.

I thought long and deep
Over years that have passed
I am not one to keep
I am unwanted trash.

12. Miss You Not

I missed you today,
I try to shake off the feeling.
Get out of my head,
get out of my heart.
I tell myself;
"He misses me, I do not miss him",
I try to trick my subconscious into submission.
You miss me,
for all those reasons that you took for granted;
my gentle loving nature,
my heartfelt encouragement,
my sincere dedication to your smile.
You will miss all of this
for a good long while.

13. End of the Line

There is something bigger than myself happening at this
moment;
bigger than anything I can assume credit for.
It was choreographed in the stars and patiently set aside
for years.
Building up steam....
Patiently waiting,
yet eagerly anticipating.
Like an ear on the rail road track;
doing nothing but listening.
Awaiting the roar of the locomotive that wooooshes by
without slowing down.
No passengers get on here.
No stops or farewells.
In a blink of an eye,
it's on its journey.
That is the way I feel concerning this huge thing about to
become what ever it is to become.
This thing that has been manifesting for decades.
The will was there,

the knowledge was accruing
and when the time arrives I will know.
For now.....
On with the show.

14. Anhelo

The way your memory creeps up into my sleep and
makes me downhearted.
I open my eyes to wonder why.
I think really hard about the last time we were together.
Intertwined whispering needs and wants quietly in a
hushed secret way.
I thought about you so deeply that I could almost feel
you.
Your lips pressed against my neck,
us kissing....
holding each other until we have to let go.
I did not know
Nor did you show
It would be the last for us both.

15. When Love Becomes Energy

Write about the things you love,
smiles that captivate you;
leaving you eagerly paralyzed in a memory.
Write about secrets that are safe with the soul that you
mourn,
about the aching of never kissing lips so soft.
Yearning for things that no longer exist is familiar to me.
Seeking that which is out of reach,
oppressing love that could not be expressed;
between you and me.
Undying that love becomes energy,
and somehow..... somewhere....
It is free.

16. Lift Me Up

I can not rely on any one
I wonder how I am doing this all on my own.
Will anyone ever love me?
Or am I sentenced to a life alone?
There is a lot to bear on these shoulders of mine,
I keep moving forward
when all I want to do is hide.
The days pass by swift
with no time to rest,
as a single parent
doing my absolute best.
I am so tired
and when it is too much
I pray to GOD to lift me up

PLEASE GOD LIFT ME UP.

17. After What You Said.....

All of a sudden those
late night laughs on the pillow meant nothing.
Chasing sunsets....
and wading waters too shallow to swim but deep enough
for you to hold me.
Contently,
we sat without words
for a silent moment.
The kind of silence
that makes a memory.
An afterthought
that will echo in your ear repeatedly.
Like the brackish tide memories
I have of you and me.

18. Depth

I crave deep cavernous types of intimacy,
the kind that most fear.
Because it is so much to bear.....
But isn't that what love does?
Bears all things....
Well bear me not.....
whilst my mind will flee...
If your shallow canals lack the depth for my buoyancy.

19. Free Myself

Break the bond
while the thread is unbound.
Nothing attaches itself very closely.
This makes it easy to break free.
There is no love....
There is no intimacy....
Nothing at all
attaching you to me.

20. I Will Dissappear

I don't know why I give you the chance to hurt me,
over and over....
I am going to close myself off.
There will be no way for you to gain access to me.
Search for me everywhere,
search far and wide
look for me in so many eyes.
Try to catch a glimpse
hoping to see,
but you will find nowhere
little ole me.

21. EROS

I believe you can love a multitude of people
a multitude of ways.
Some for a short while
some never fades;
persisting in a young woman's heart
until the day her breath and body do part.

(Dedicated to Michael "ERO" Stapleton
May you rest in peace)